ULSTER POEM
Featuring Local Writers

GH00367334

Published by
Drumlamph Books
Matt & Sarah Bruce
Walnut Cottage, 46 Killyberry Road
Bellaghy, Magherafelt. BT45 8LJ

Collectors
John Hughes, Richard Frew and Matthew T Bruce

Editor
Richard Frew

ISBN: 0-9550149-0-5

Front Cover: New Bridge, Toomebridge
Photograph by George McIntyre

Acknowledgements

The compilers of this anthology would like to express our gratitude to all those who provided assistance in the production of this work, in particular those present day writers who donated their work so willingly and also the families and representatives of those writers who have past away, some many years ago.

In addition thanks are also due to those who assisted in other ways and without whose support this work would not have been possible.

Ms Patsy Horton, Blackstaff Press
Paddy Donnelly, Australia formerly Bellaghy
Fr Pat Crilly, Desertmartin
Graham Mawhinney, Draperstown
Jim & Mrs Rose Walsh, Ballymacpeake
Hugh Bradley, Upperlands
George McIntyre, Cookstown
Robert Mawhinney, Castledawson
Clr George Shiels, Maghera
Mrs Mary McEldowney, Swatragh
Mrs Gretta Junkin, Bellaghy
Mrs Josephine Sloss, Maghera
Mrs Ann Kilpatrick, Toomebridge
Frank Dale, Toomebridge
John Stewart, Toomebridge
Ms Marie McCann, Toomebridge
Brian McCann, Toomebridge
John Hurl, Toomebridge
John Kennedy, Cullybackey
Mr & Mrs J W Abbott, Ahoghill
Mrs Margaret Henry, Tobermore
Cllr John Junkin, Portglenone

Foreword

I am delighted that so much is being done in our area to portray the native culture and tradition of Ulster through poetry, and I wish to commend Richard Frew and Matthew Bruce for their efforts to preserve the past. 'Ulster Poems 2005' is an example of what can be done to preserve our cultural heritage. Each poem in this Anthology helps to define our landscape and convey the fabric of our local history.

We often forget that everyday happenings are history and the fact that these poems make reference to local events and people mean they are an invaluable source of material to chart social history. What is more, the sense of pride and identity which is generated by the knowledge of one's own community is something we can pass on to our most treasured possession, our children.

Ray Graham
3 March 2005

Introduction

It is with pleasure that I write an introduction to this anthology of verse, 'Ulster Poems 2005'. The poets concerned are following in noble footsteps, keeping alive a tradition dating back to the 5th century, when the last great pagan bard 'Torna' died.

Down the centuries poetry has been an enjoyable experience for both composer and reader. Our forebears enriched their lives through learning verse, putting it to good use in improving their speech and sharpening their ability to find the apt phrase when needed. They also retained many of the values contained in the poems and more importantly passed them on to future generations.

The reader will find the poems have a local flavour having been written by people from Counties Antrim, Derry and Tyrone. They describe most facets of country and urban life, while demonstrating the wealth of material that exists in the area.

In reading the poems we are taken on a poetic journey throughout the area. In the course of which we meet the flax scutcher's son in a poem 'The Lad' written by W F Marshall. We visit George Barnett's country near Draperstown then enjoy Hugh Connors experience buying and selling livestock in Larkin's auction ring in Magherafelt.

The reading of Robin Crilly's poem takes us to Curran fair and Ballynahone Moss, (now saved from extinction). We journey on to the Creagh Airfield and experience what it was like to live there 60 years ago when it was operational. Owen Toal's poem lets us view the homes of Moneyglass, as we travel through Cargin and on to Randalstown.

The next port of call is Ballymena where we get a whiff of what it was like to work in a dusty old mill in times past, before going to visit the surrounding area. Then it's time to meet the business people of Cullybackey and others in that locality, before taking the road to

Portglenone and Clady and enjoying verse in praise of those places, the rivers Bann and The Clady, not forgetting Mullaghnamoyagh Hill. We continue through to Aghadowey and Swatragh areas, there we are introduced to the girls of Moneysharvin. On our way through the Parish of Lavey we pay a visit to the bogs of Mayogall where turf are being footed, before journeying on to Bellaghy and Jean Bell's well close to what was once the 'Shillin Hill' where the journey ends.

On our travels we have recalled schooldays and many other pastimes, from the game of marbles to dancing in halls. The journey now completed the hope is that it was an enjoyable one and that the readers will agree that the compilers of the book, Matt Bruce and Richard Frew are to be congratulated and thanked for their efforts in bringing this project to a successful conclusion. To collect, type and edit in excess of 60 poems required a great deal of time and effort, not to mention the many other publishing hurdles that must be got over before success was achieved.

John Hughes
23 February 2005

Index

The Old Thatched Cottage

It was just an old thatched cottage,
at the bottom of our street.
Years ago it was a home,
a place to eat and sleep.

A turf fire burning in the hearth,
to give off welcome heat.
In the old thatched cottage,
at the bottom of the street.

The windows there were very small,
it had the old half door.
People in those early days,
never looked for more.

They did not long for riches,
or foreign lands to roam.
All the people wanted then,
was a place to call their home.

Prosperity has come along,
the world is changing fast.
Soon the old thatched cottage
will be a thing of the past.

New houses soon will take its place,
the past becomes a dream.
All is left is a gaping hole,
where the old thatched cottage has been.

Developers have moved in,
and taken it away.
The last old thatched cottage,
we had here in Kilrea.

Andy Alexander
Kilrea

An Ulster Emigrant

'Twas on a bright May morning,
in nineteen fifty two.
I left my home in Antrim,
a new life to pursue.

My dear old mother stood there,
a teardrop in her eye.
To leave her almost broke my heart,
a new life I had to try.

The work was scarce and times were hard,
money was in short supply.
So I packed all my possessions,
and bid my friends goodbye.

From Belfast harbour I set sail,
my heart was sad and sore.
To leave my native land behind,
for a far off distant shore.

I stood on deck and slowly watched,
the coastline disappear.
And when it all had vanished,
I shed a silent tear.

When I reached my destination,
I was weary, tired and worn.
No one to share my troubles with,
I was really on my own.

My first job was a farm hand,
and worked from dawn till dusk.
I had made my own decision now,
and hard work was a must.

My mother often wondered,
how I was getting on.
She always prayed to God above,
to keep her darling son.

The years passed by and soon I knew,
this life is not for me.
But I couldn't forget my dear old home,
and all my family.

I often sat and wondered,
about my life serene.
When you read this little poem,
you may know just who I mean.

Nan Anderson
July 1995
Cullybackey

The Angels

I've often heard great clergy preach,
in days long since gone by.
And pictured wondrous angel hosts,
which seemed to dwell on high.
But though I've searched the starry skies,
for many's the weary year.
I never saw an angel there,
amongst the starry spheres.

But trouble reached my home at last,
and grief and pain I felt.
Till in the District Hospital,
I lay in Magherafelt.
But grief gave place to hope at last,
and banished was despair.
When I beheld before my eyes,
a lot of Angels there.

They had white veils upon their heads,
with dresses of the same.
Which differed somewhat in degree,
strict order to maintain.
But there was an angelic look,
upon each smiling face.
As they brought hope through every ward,
to many a doubtful case.

They soothed the ill, they helped the weak,
and eased the ones in pain.
And all who look to them for aid,
do never seek in vain.
For each has an appointed task,
the high ones and the low.
And each performs their duty well,
as through the wards they go.

And still the preachers come and go,
to talk, to preach, to pray.
And still they think of angel throngs,
that's somehow far away.
But I'll no longer search the skies,
or think of distant spheres.
For Heaven's in Co Derry,
as we have the Angels here.

Geordie Barnett
(1876-1965)
Draperstown

Bogs Of Mayogall

On the twenty-fifth of June in the afternoon
The weather was somewhat cold.
I did intend to meet a friend
So off to the bogs I strolled.
The heather in bloom had a sweet perfume
The trees so green and tall,
There I spied two sweets there winning peats
In the Bogs of Mayogall.

I gently slipped up to them
I bid them time of day
They asked me had I lost myself
Or where did I mean to stray.
I said I had an appointment with
A friend that was to call.
To meet a chum I just had come
To the Bogs of Mayogall.

I stood and viewed those heathery banks
Where I stood in days of yore.
With comrades gay that are far away
And in another shore.
My heart's inclined to keep in mind
The rolling of the ball.
That night so sweet with the heather bleat
In the Bogs of Mayogall.

So then Miss G she said to me
Would you put up a few.
I said, I would, she said that's good.
I surely will help you
I joked and smoked
And spent the day to the dark began to fall.
At half-past ten they were all on their end
In the Bogs of Mayogall.

So then Miss G she made the tea
We all sat down to dine.
In Heather View Hotel that night
We spent a pleasant time.
Our table was a mossy bank
With rush bushes large and small.
We spent some hours amongst the flowers
In the Bogs of Mayogall.

Our feathered friend the water hen
Came out a run to see
All through the marshy bog holes
As angry as could be.
The little cheeper on the twig
It seemed to scold us one and all.
It seemed to say to get away
From the Bogs of Mayogall.

Then Miss C likewise Miss G
They bundled up the ware.
At eleven o'clock called summer-time
For home we did prepare.
It was a blooming picnic
And one I will recall.
May we all live to hear the bleat next year
In the Bogs of Mayogall.

So my lovely hens my lady friends
I'll bid you all adieu.
We parted on the D-crossroads
And homeward did pursue.
The evening sun had hid itself
Behind your mountain tall,
So I bid adieu to you
And the Bogs of Mayogall.

Willie Bradley
(1889-1957)
Upperlands

Big John the Whistler

There are people with great talent,
here within our Emerald Isle.
Musicians, singers, dancers too,
of elegance and style.

But when it comes to whistling,
one performer stands alone.
And his name is John O'Connell,
the big man from Portglenone.

All over towns and villages,
across this fair North Land.
His whistling has resounded,
with a rhythm pure and grand.

With reel and jig and hornpipe,
his fame is widely known.
For he's Ulster's greatest whistler,
big John from Portglenone.

'Tis many years he's whistled now,
at session and Fleadh Cheoil.
From Belfast to Kilkenny,
and from Sligo to Listowel.

In many other places too,
both near and far from home.
The lively airs are much admired,
of big John from Portglenone.

In the year of nineteen ninety,
he won in Antrim too.
With a fine display of whistling,
sure his equals there are few.

At the Ulster Fleadh in Warrenpoint,
his genius it was shown.
When he was declared the champion there,
big John from Portglenone.

Then here's to this great whistler,
who has really stood the test.
And to his friends in Antrim too,
we wish them all the best.

When next he visits Limerick West,
we'll treat him like our own.
With a welcome that is fitting for,
big John from Portglenone.

Pat Brosnan

Food For Thought

These days it seems there's such a fuss,
About which foods are bad for us:
What's worse I notice with dismay
The list grown longer every day.
They're all the things I like the most
Yorkshire Pudding, Sunday roast.

Toast with butter thickly spread,
Home-made jam on fresh brown bread.
What about pavlova with lots of cream?
Sure every bite is just a dream.
Cheese and paté are suspect too
I really don't know what to do.

Chicken and pork I'm advised not to eat,
So I think O.K. I'll have a nice bit of meat,
But no - I might catch this BSE,
And that could be the end of me.
I'm a nervous wreck - what'll I do?
A strong cup of coffee - will that kill me too.

In days gone by if you didn't feel good;
A tummy upset - off your food:
A soft-boiled egg or a pudding made of milk
Just the thing to get you back in the 'pink'
But now cholesterol, salmonella, is all you hear
And your soft-boiled egg has to be hard, I fear.

Obediently, when I was small
What mother served I ate it all:
It seems to me that now I'm old,
I still must eat what I am told.
But, since everything I ate was wrong,
I marvel that I've lived this long.

Doreen Brown
Moneymore

Ode To The Black Bull

A statistic, a fact, a pub that's burned down,
in the Co Antrim village of Randalstown.
These were the headlines in paper and news,
leaving many people with different views.

Was it them or us or just done for a lark,
or faulty electrics that ignited a spark.
The Black Bull for many was a way of life,
holding together through our years of strife.

My memories of the Bull are long and are fond,
and to far distant days I often abscond.
With a bottle of Guinness, a cigarette,
and a game of darts for a sixpenny bet.

Celebrating a birthday, a night with no end,
drowning our sorrows, farewell to a friend.
A quiet drink, down under the stairs,
chatting away all our worries and cares.

If no-one was in you could turn back the clock,
and those drab old walls would whisper and talk.
whether one sort or another or from near or far,
harmony and friendship could be found at the bar.

When firemen left that old blackened shell,
a million memories had gone as well.
But the old pub had a warm beating heart,
let's hope for the future that it doesn't depart.

David Burrows
Randalstown

The Hills of Garriffgeery

It was in my youthful boyhood days,
that I made up my mind.
To pack a few belongings,
and leave my friends behind.

I crossed the wide Atlantic,
to Alaska I was bound.
A Klondyke miner told me,
there was gold below the ground.

It took me two weeks travelling,
I was thinking every day.
About the hills of Garriffgeery,
and my homeland far away.

On June the eighth I landed there,
tough men were standing round.
I knew whenever I spoke to them,
they worked below the ground.

Their faces were unshaven,
they had braved the winter's cold.
They came out there the same as me,
in search of precious gold.

So as I stood and listened,
I heard one old man say.
The lads from Garriffgeery,
in old Ireland far away.

I walked about for three long weeks,
before I got a job.
I started with a blacksmith,
and they called him "one blow Bob".

He was a happy tradesman,
I loved to hear him sing.
When I reached him red hot irons,
he made the anvil ring.

After I had worked a week,
I was handed out my pay.
So I sent some to my mother dear,
in old Ireland far away.

The mountains in the springtime,
were a lovely shade of green.
You could see the brown bears feeding there,
and hear the wolverene.

There were lots of grouse and tamagin,
running round the woods.
They worked hard all the summer days,
attending to their broods.

The coyotes growled away all night,
their echo seemed to say.
Go back to Garriffgeery,
in old Ireland far away.

When autumn winds are blowing,
you can smell the coming snow.
The frost set in, and temperatures,
are twenty-five below.

The old brown bear has disappeared,
into his lonely den.
It will be the month of May next year,
when you see him out again.

I dreaded the long winter months,
but longing for the day.
I'd see old Garriffgeery,
and my hills so far away.

It was on one cold October day,
that I made up my mind.
To pack my few belongings,
and leave this land behind.

I glanced up at the mountains,
I viewed the rugged plain.
I saw those tough old miners,
that I'd never see again.

The siren it was blowing,
the boat was in the bay.
I'll head for Garriffgeery,
in old Ireland far away.

Next morning at the dock-side,
old pals were standing by.
Whenever I shook their hands I saw,
the teardrops in their eye.

I had not made much money,
I did not stake a claim.
But they shouted out in chorus,
"will ye no come back again".

And as I stood upon the deck,
I heard one old man say.
The lad's for Garriffgeery,
and his homeland far away.

**Hugh Carey
(1903-1995)
Randalstown**

My Poem Just For Mum

How do you tell a Mother
Just how really much she's loved
Words in a card or a prayer
Or maybe just a hug.

If I say 'Mum' it seems too vague
To show how much you do
The work, the pain, the worry
That a Mum alone goes through.

No gift on earth is worthy
Of how much to me she means
Everything she's done and said,
An endless list it seems.

You're always there to give me love
My companion, soulmate, friend
You're always there to listen,
And all my pains to mend.

If only she could read my heart
To know just how I feel
Nothing else can equal
Those feelings now revealed.

I can only say "I love you"
Which comes straight from the heart
You're always there beside me
Your spirit n'er to part.

Not only are you Mum to me
But a vital piece of my heart
The one who makes me so complete
Who's been there from the start.

I hope this poem has said it all
To you this special day
Exactly what you mean to me
Which I can not repay.

A final word of thanks to you
My very special Mum
No one will ever take your place
To me your number one.

Elaine Clarke
Castledawson

Ballynease in Spring

I wish that I could walk again,
beneath those spreading trees.
Along a lovely country road,
in dear old Ballynease.

The laurels green, laburnum's cream,
the hawthorn pink and red.
The fragrant honeysuckle,
in coloured beauty spread.

So lovely and appealing,
who could their freshness scorn.
Their blended colours pretty look,
upon a Spring-like morn.

Those flowers sweet all bloom again,
each blooming branch doth swing.
And every bud unfolds a leaf,
to welcome back the spring.

The modest primrose wakes again,
the daisies peeping through.
The daffodils bow down their heads,
to crocus white and blue.

The birds do join in chorus,
with mingled notes to sing.
Oh! what a glorious season,
is each returning spring.

The swallow wings its message,
that summer's in the air.
The butterfly and buzzing bee,
have not a single care.

To hear the cuckoo's call again,
that makes the beech groves ring.
To watch the lark soar up on high,
or hear the mavis sing.

To see the sunshine strike at noon,
the dew upon the grass.
To see those pretty shots again,
or e'er this life doth pass.

Oh! would that I could these glories see,
when all the earth is still.
Just when the sun is peeping forth,
atop of Tully Hill.

With all these happy thoughts of spring,
my heart it's joy hath said.
Alas, those dearly cherished scenes,
now from my sight have fled.

Jennie Colquhoun
(1897-1951)
Portglenone/Canada

Will

At my demise let all be wise,
let there be no complaining.
My debts that's just, pay them all first,
I leave then what's remaining.

To my wife Ann and all my land,
my crops, my goods, my chattles.
For her to give and to divide,
when her affairs she settles.

As matter runs, my own two sons,
the land they'll maybe claim it.
That's subject to a mortgage due,
if fit for to redeem it.

Well if you like I don't object,
that's if you think they'll keep it.
And cultivate it up to date,
and plough and sow and reap it.

Hold your control over the whole,
advice to you I'm giving.
And keep the home to be your own,
as long as you are living.

Nineteen hundred and twenty eight,
is the year let it be noted.
This eighth of June, I George Colquhoun,
with my own hand have wrote it.

George Colquhoun
(1849-1935)
Portglenone

TV

My grandchildren often ask me,
as they gather around my knee.
Gran please tell us a story,
of just how things used to be.

Away back in the olden days,
when you were young and free.
Life must have been so boring then,
in the years before TV.

Ah children dear come listen here,
and I'll tell you how things were.
Away back in the olden days,
when I was just a little girl.

Sure we didn't know what boredom meant,
we made our own fun then you see.
It was a sad day for the human race,
when they introduced TV.

Sure you'll never know the fun we had,
when we climbed the chestnut tree.
To find the biggest chestnut there,
for all our friends to see.

Or gather in the evening,
around the auld Mill Brook.
To try and catch a fish or two,
with a stick and a fishing hook.

Sure you never had the pleasure,
on a long hot summers day.
Of running barefoot through the meadow,
where we tossed the new mown hay.

Or help the farmer tramp the lint,
into the water dam.
To be rewarded by the farmer's wife,
with a piece of bread and jam.

You have never heard the corncrake,
on a sunny summer's morn.
Nor have you ever seen the reaper,
mowing down the yellow corn.

Or see them stack the sheaves of corn,
that was a sight to see.
But alas we'll see these sights no more,
'twas long before TV.

Ah children sure my heart is sore,
for your sad and empty lives.
You were born into a wicked world,
of bigotry and strife.

You will have no tales to tell your grandchildren,
when you're old and grey like me.
They stole your childhood years away,
when they introduced TV.

Phyllis Conway
Plumbridge

Memories Of The Moss

I will tell you a story
Of the times I used to know,
How the people spent their time
In the days of long ago.
From Ballymoughan and Coolshinney,
Dunamoney and Caraloon
They came to Ballinahone
In the months of May and June.

There was no class distinction,
The workman and his boss,
And all the local people
Were heading for the moss.
All kinds of people
With their barrow and their spade,
The 'Doctor' and the 'Clergy'
Were there to render aid.

We had to light a fire
And put the kettle on,
No better cure for hunger
Than a big griddle scone.
Plenty of crack as we sat at the stack,
We enjoyed it just as well
As a cushioned seat and a fancy place
In a Grade A hotel.

A snail in the spout of the kettle,
I can't tell how it got in,
When we finished the tay, there it lay,
In the bottom of Charlie's tin.
If you want a drink of water,
You can freely drink your fill,
There is no doubt, it came from the spout
At the foot of Anderson's hill.

If you haven't got the time
Or your watch is going slow,
When you hear the train come through the Grange,
Hide the tools and go.
Cutting turf is thirsty,
Yet you won't hear them complain,
When you're on your way at the end of the day,
Call in with Davy or Jane.

Going home one evening
With the basket and tin can,
We met some Scottish visitors
Who quickly turned and ran.
They didn't wait to investigate,
For someone heard them say
"What a terrible crowd of tinkers,
We had better run away".

The moss road is now deserted,
And the carts have gone for good.
Trees and bushes are growing
Where the turf castles stood.
I once went back to see the moss
And thought of days gone by
When we cut the turf and chatted
As we spread them out to dry.

With no turf-stack to rest my back,
I was standing there alone
Admiring the purple heather
In the bogs of Ballinahone.
Most of the moss-men are gone now,
And only a few remain,
We need some more to take their place
Good men like Andy Kane.

Robert J Crilly
(1905-1997)
Rocktown

The Star Of Williie Strathern

On the road to Castledawson,
as you leave Bellaghy Town.
Lies the spread of Killyberry,
sanctified in deep renown.
From among its' fern and bracken,
came a youth now steeped in fame.
He was one of Wolf Tone's greatest,
Willie Strathern was his name.

I remember well our school boy days,
with the war in Europe gone.
While the scars of Ireland's tortured past,
were doomed to linger on.
I still dwell upon those long gone days,
and even more with joy.
When memory heeds the sporting deeds,
of the Killyberry boy.

And the star of Willie Strathern,
will forever shine above.
Spreading beams of inspiration,
shedding rays of hope and love.
In the blue and white he was a sight,
as comrades will recall.
As he outclassed champions of his time,
and never dropped a ball.

The late fifties and the sixties,
witnessed Willie at his best.
As he soared on high as eagles fly,
to reach their mountain crest.
And when games were tight there was no fright,
instead a measured laugh.

When you saw the Killyberry man,
stand tall at centre half.

Though oft the rough and tumble reigned,
he never left his post.
He stood with pride, ne'er stepped aside,
and gave much more than most.
And I thank God on this foreign sod,
for giving me the joy.
To have worn the blue with comrades true,
like the Killyberry boy.

And none can say to this present day,
was brave Willie tested more.
Than when fate decreed through a tragic deed,
brother Johnny's life was o'er.
He nearly lost his own life then,
but on everyone's behalf.
He returned again to Wolfe Tone's men,
to his spot at centre half.

Once again he starred and the foe was barred,
from infringing on his den.
By his side there stood, as well they should,
the rest of Wolfe Tone's men.
And again he tried while loved ones cried,
fond tears of love and joy.
Delighting in the graceful spin,
of the Killyberry boy.

Paddy Donnelly
Bellaghy/Australia

The Village

Most people have heard of Bellaghy
For we've been in the news quite a lot.
Our wee village is well worth a visit
It's amazing the potential it's got.

The Manor, now the Police Station
So impressive with lights all around.
They say there's an underground tunnel
Which connects with the Bawn on the mound.

Retracing our steps into history
When battles were fought by the score.
The Bawn or the fortified farm house
Was a haven for both rich and poor.

To-day it's a centre of culture
Where people can browse at their will.
The talent displayed has been honoured worldwide
Heaney's works are top of the bill.

Along Castle Street is a house named 'Bawn Lodge'
Where guests are welcome to stay.
The food cooked and served by Mary Lou Todd
Is top of the range, so they say.

The shops are all packed full of goodies
You are sure of a bargain no doubt.
There's the VG, the Chemist's and Kearney's
Overlooking our new roundabout.

People think we are all gospel greedy
Five churches we have to our name.
Presbyterian, Baptist and Brethren
St Mary's and the Church down the lane.

We have two schools in this little village
One maintained the other controlled.
With our children divided right from the start
There are sad repercussions untold.

If you like to relax with a good book
Then the Library can supply all you need.
There are books of all kinds and descriptions
For those who are willing to read.

We've a Medical Centre in our village
You go there the doctor to see.
Then take your prescription to Michael
He'll exchange it for a small fee.

As you make your way out of the village
Certain houses come into view
There's the Manse, the Parochial and the Rectory
Occupied by the selected few.

You know we are really quite privileged
With all these amenities at hand.
Why then must there be so much disquiet
In this part of our dear little land?

Margaret Evans
Bellaghy

Unexpected

Kenneth's birthday had arrived,
and he pondered where he'd go.
To celebrate with all his friends,
now he'd hit the big four 0.

He thought about that disco club,
he'd been to once last year.
The very pretty girl he'd met,
and shed a silent tear.

He recalled how unexpectedly,
when their eyes met just by chance.
He walked across that maple floor,
and asked the girl to dance.

She said her name was Susan,
and he told her he was Ken.
He judged she'd be about a nine,
on a scale of one to ten.

Kenneth didn't have much luck,
with the other girls he'd met.
But he thought she might be different,
although he didn't know that yet.

He reckoned things were going well,
as they danced the night away.
Perhaps he'd ask to take her home,
to hear what she would say.

He told her that her beauty was,
so far beyond compare.
And he was really blown away,
by her locks of golden hair.

Before he spoke again he felt,
a pain like none before.
And blacked out for a moment,
as he crumpled to the floor.

The darkness slowly lifted and,
the blur began to clear.
To get this matter figured out,
he'd need his brain in gear.

At first he saw the size fourteens,
then the big shock of his life.
When a man of six foot seven said,
keep your hands off my wife.

Richard Frew
Bellaghy

Mosside Ladies Meeting

There was hubbub and excitement,
In Mosside Hall last night.
When the ladies of the congregation,
Met with one aim in their sight.

To make a lot of money quick,
And clear their debts away.
So we all put on our thinking caps,
About functions that would pay.

The first thing then that sprang to mind,
Was good Saint Patrick's Day.
We'd hold a feast with Irish Stew,
And ask our friends to stay.

We'd follow this with apple tart,
Lashings of cream as well.
Then tea and biscuits, what a treat,
We hope t'will turn out swell.

A programme there will have to be,
With song and dance and poetry.
Jokes and rhymes and fancy dress,
The choir will surely you impress.

Dressed in green from head to feet,
Their Irish airs will be so sweet.
And when you listen you'll hear the beat,
As tap, tap, tapping go your feet.

We'll get the tickets printed soon,
And hope our friends will come.
To support us in our effort,
And join in all the fun.

The ladies sure, will serve you well,
With no fuss, or no delay.
And bring your tickets when you come,
Or at the door you'll pay.

We look forward to the 17th,
We hope the night is fine.
We look forward to the fellowship,
With friends from every clime.

We look forward to a jolly time,
Forgetting the wind and weather.
Leaving our cares and woes behind,
And enjoying the night together.

Margaret Getty
Mosside

Thoughts of a Rustic

Hawthorn hedges bright with berries,
distant hills outlined against the sky.
Sunshine stealing through the woodlands,
fox's yelp and curlews cry.

Gossamer on autumn mornings,
reapers wake of new-mown hay.
Pigeons cooing in the ivy,
wild ducks call at break of day.

Pastures green, cattle peacefully grazing,
corncrake calling in a field nearby.
Long leg heron in the shallows gazing,
Kestral hovering in the midday sky.

Once deep set in trusted country ways,
it's impossible to ever break the habit.
Like walking by a pool at evening flight,
or purse nets set to catch a timid rabbit.

These are thoughts alive with happy memories,
and in the country keep me free from care.
But I'm a naturalist at heart, and all I ask,
is God's clean country air.

Brian Grant
Toomebridge

Ode to the Bard of Bellaghy

Billy Leonard the Bard of Bellaghy,
(Near neighbour of Heaney you know)
For between them there's only the distance,
Of a mile by the flight of a crow.

Boul Seamus he wrote of the boglands
And travelled far over the earth.
But I wonder tonight is he missing,
The poteen and peat round the hearth.

Ach, though one is both famous and clever,
And his poems read by folks far away.
His loss to Bellaghy is countered,
By one who decided to stay.

Not famous as yet is this poet,
Who writes of O'Neill and Maguire.
But it's you, Billy Leonard we're praising,
As we read your poems here by the fire.

There are plenty who put words together,
On Ireland, her rivers and land.
But few who can write of her people,
With the gift of the gab at your hand.

Once more to "The Bard of Bellaghy",
I raise a cup of good cheer.
More power to your elbow, Boul William,
And make sure your still's running clear.

Dennis Greig
Belfast

The Plantation

The plantation is a formation of trees,
a habitat for the birds and bees.
A shelter from the wind and rain,
when trees come into leaf again.

These stately trees so tall and green,
stand erect and so serene.
Inviting birds to build their nests,
to lay their eggs and take a rest.

It really is a bird's building site,
for the crow and wild pigeon alike.
Or any other birds who choose,
to build their nests on those leafy boughs.

The plantation isn't for beauty alone,
it has many other purposes as well.
Along comes the wood cutter one day,
and decides which ones he will fell.

Some are chopped up for firewood,
others are pulped for paper.
Some are used to make furniture,
and are put through many a caper.

These trees are something special,
with their forty shades of green.
Mother nature is so wonderful,
to provide us with this scene.

Bessie Hanna
Cullybackey

Equality

When women won the right to vote,
"we're equal!" they all shouted.
A woman equal to a man?
she might be, but I doubt it.

For with the passing of the years,
there comes the telling signs.
Crow's feet around a woman's eyes,
a man gets laughter lines.

And if he's fashion conscious,
he's just a well dressed man.
If a woman keeps up with the times,
she's mutton dressed as lamb.

And when a man gets silver streaks,
running through his hair.
He's considered quite alluring,
mature and debonair.

But when the grey begins to show,
in a woman's crowning glory.
Forget about attractive,
for it's quite a different story.

And when she gains an ounce or two,
she's burdened down with guilt.
While he can put on pounds and still,
be handsome and well built.

And what about the eyesight,
when it begins to fade.
A pair of gold rimmed glasses,
and he's really got it made.

The woman - well - she's getting on,
when her vision's not so good.
It's time she took things easy,
she'd like to if she could.

But what about the housework,
the fight with dust and dirt.
It has to be attended to,
but that is woman's work.

Equality? Where did it go?
when you stop to think about it.
A woman equal to a man?
she might be, but I doubt it.

Betty Hueston
Portglenone

The Aerodrome Site

I have mingled with mortals from princes to tramps,
I have slept in fine castles, in cow sheds and camps.
I have lived in the jungle with monkey and apes,
wild beasts and vile reptiles all sizes and shapes.

Yet wherever I wandered I always could find,
some rest for my body, some peace of mind.
Till an ill-natured fate in a spasm of spite,
condemned me to live on an aerodrome site.

Here are the huts by the hundred and sheds by the score,
weird buildings of brickwork and concrete galore.
So odd and so ugly you'd think them designed,
by a practical joker astray in the mind.

But I think of the fields that lay fair to the eye,
on the broad of their backs laughing up at the sky.
And the homes that were pictures of peace and delight,
now levelled and lost in an aerodrome site.

There are planes on the ground, there are planes in the air,
and the racket they raise would make a clergyman swear.
With the roar and the blast of the engines combined,
in a nerve wrecking tempest of thunder and wind.

It staggers the trees till they double and break,
it scatters the fishing boats over the lake.
And ghosts from the graveyard appear in the night,
aroused by the roar of the aerodrome site.

The highways and byways with Yankees abound,
in jeeps and on cycles careering around.
Tough guys from Chicago, swell lads from New York,
their fathers from Finland, their mothers from Cork.

Tight cowboys from Texas, stout ranchers from Maine,
their mothers from Moscow, their fathers from Spain
All types of races, brown, yellow and white.
all loose and at large on the aerodrome site.

At daybreak our tempers are put to the test,
by the blare of a bugle that shatters our rest.
And rouses the regiments of old Uncle Sam
who bound from their beds with a stout, hearty damn.

Then out rush the busses, the vans and the jeeps,
with a crash and a clatter that gives you the creeps.
Why the doctors declare there is nobody right,
who has lived for a month on an aerodrome site.

By the time you've got used to this wild carry-on,
you're as deaf as a post and your reason is gone.
You behave like a bull that has seen a red rag,
every time you look up at the Star Spangled Flag.

I have always believed, and I'll always maintain,
'twas the devil himself who invented the plane.
You may say that I'm wrong, but you'll swear that I'm right,
if you happen to live on an aerodrome site.

Stop Press

A message has reached me since starting my tale,
the Yanks are preparing for hitting the trail.
And I feel rather sorry, for freely I own,
more kind hearted fellows I never have known.

But though they are bound for the front of the fray,
where there's wild, wicked slaughter by night and by day.
Where battles are raging by day and by night,
it should make a nice change from an aerodrome site.

Michael Hurl
Newbridge

Autumn in Carndaisy Glen

Winter frosts have come and gone,
Spring has been and flowers have grown.
And how the summer's really flown,
And now it's the autumn time.

There a hundred shades of brown,
And leaves are lying all around.
The evenings are really darkening down,
Because it's the autumn time.

The swallow we do see no more,
Winter's knock is at the door.
And the rain and wind I do deplore,
In the autumn time.

Children reach around the chestnut tree,
To find the nuts that has fallen free.
There's going to be a conker spree,
This autumn time.

The rowan holds its berries high,
While beech nuts fall to ground and lie,
They're all food to a pigeons eye,
In the autumn time.

Mulberries grow and rosehips too,
Orange and red their separate hue.
Are there many? No just a few,
This autumn time.

Haw and holly have berries red,
Sloe and damson are black instead.
Yet the Lord makes sure the birds are fed,
In the autumn time.

The plum tree also has its fruit,
While squirrels, acorns from the oak tree loot.
Storing God's provisions their pursuit,
In the autumn time.

Blackberries hang brown, black and red,
Among a multitude of spiders webs.
As their end of cycle closer ebbs,
In the autumn time.

Now may I take this occasion?
To ask you what's the reason.
That God has made this special season,
This autumn time.

I believe there's a message there,
Just as for winter you must prepare.
Without God's salvation how would fair,
In life's autumn time.

Accept God's provision repent of sin,
And let the King of glory in.
Then in life or death you will win,
with the Lord of autumn time.

Tom Johnston
Moneymore

Restless Be The Wind And Me

Oh! listen to the dripping rain,
as it patters on the window pane.
And the weird wind moans like an evil one,
as I sit alone for the morning sun.

Oh! restless wind, its you I'm like,
you're not content by day or night.
You will not settle to haunt or home,
and I was also born to roam.

To roam this place that's made for me,
to travel far to learn and see.
To see his wonders he gives me lease,
when this is done I find my peace.

As the rivers rush to the restless sea,
or the honey searched for by the bee.
Vagabond! fortune hunter! call at me,
my mind's made up, a rambler to be.

Seamus Keenan
Randalstown

The Cottage of my Fathers'

Far up in yonder valley,
where the infant stream is born.
Where the mist descends the mountain,
and the moorfowl wakes the morn.

Where the deep recesses darken,
and the crags are old and grey.
Overhung with blossomed woodbines,
bending neath the silvery spray.

Stands the cottage of my fathers,
in a neat and trimly spot.
Graced by all the hallowed memories,
of an Irish peasant's cot.

Sheltered by its' hoary ash trees,
towering in the midway air.
How I envied all their gladness,
to the birds when singing there.

Underneath its' aged rooftree,
many a wholesome board was spread.
Many a festive harvest gathering,
speak of years long past and fled.

There the old loved songs of Erin,
sounded by the peat fire's glow.
And their wild enchanting sweetness,
made the heart forget its' woe.

Patriot strains and Christmas anthems,
in the old and rustic style.
Blushing love and dauntless valour,
of the heart-loved native isle.

There the weary sick insurgent,
found a cheerer for his fate.
In the aimless insurrection,
of the troubled ninety-eight.

Children played around its porches,
that are gone with age away.
To the great uncharted country,
whither none can tell the way.

Still the cottage stands unbroken,
through the lapse of time and tears.
And it bears the same appearance,
after nigh two hundred years.

There my sisters and my brothers,
passed our early years away.
Gathering wild fruits by the mountain,
sporting where the eddies play.

Though I've now grown to manhood,
and afar I've had to roam.
'Tis a pleasure to be thinking,
of our happy Irish home.

**John 'Paul' Kelly
(1884-1944)
Draperstown**

An Exile's Lament For His Native Land

There's a place in dear old Ireland,
where the moonbeams dance with joy.
And the pleasant river meanders,
as when I was a boy.

Not knowing what to call it,
the anglers whispered 'Toome'.
Even yet I think I see it,
with its mantels grey and green.

Along the pleasant fields of Feevagh,
and the ploughed drills straight and long.
Where the farmer steered the horse team,
and the songbird sang its song.

That small and homely village,
with its three shops and hotel.
Newsagent, mobile butcher,
and Post Office too as well.

On the River Bann the fisherman,
with his nets and hooks and all.
Caught many's the eel and salmon too,
I still can see them all.

Where they know no sin nor sorrow,
neither grief, nor strife nor pain.
I'd give the world and much much more,
to teach in Brae school again.

Down the short lane, off the main road,
I paced it twice a day.
From the school window one could see,
the Sperrin mountains far away.

On Lough Neagh's banks one morning,
the schoolchildren assembled 'round.
We headed for Scaby Island,
and darn well near' got drowned.

For such was my love of water,
I'd sit there by the shore.
At even' time when school was done,
but those days I'll see no more.

For I'm teaching now in New South Wales,
'cos ambition lured me on.
Old Toomebridge, how I think of thee,
'twill haunt me e'er I'm gone.

One last hope, and that hope is mine,
that my wish be fulfilled.
To sleep the everlasting sleep,
near Toome's beloved hills.

Alice Kelly
Rostrevor

Flamingo

I know one, no Dance Hall dandy,
and his name is S D Barr.
Built a Ballroom, called Flamingo,
spot 'twas famed, both near and far.

Came there ones who were world famous,
had the prowess with the beat.
Singing, swinging, twisting, jiving,
they could set a-dancing feet.

Twenty one years it's been going,
drawing crowds from near and far.
Prophets said, 'twould be a failure,
not so thought prudent S D Barr.

Honest, simple, unobtrusive,
has a flair that you can tell.
Expertise, he does promotions,
S D backed they all do well.

Ballymena was his birthplace,
for him here life's race began.
Sure the S we know for Sammy,
and the D's for Davidson.

Now the Ballroom will be closing,
as a Dance Hall anyway.
For the Church next door has bought it,
they'll refrain from that I'd say.

Still it's great to see them caring,
more to life than sleep and prayer.
And if harps you'd play in Heaven,
then on earth let down your hair.

Yes, Christ Jesus died to save us,
God's word doth that truth advance.
Written, too, within its pages,
we read there, a time to dance.

So although Flamingo's closing,
as the Ballroom that we knew.
May we long hear strains of music,
charm that's old, yet always new.

Let the Church fulfil her mission,
to advance God's Kingdom here.
Time to dance, time for refraining,
thanks to God that's not yet here.

Ah! Flamingo don't go winging,
blood red banner 'cross the sky.
Stay, for youth is ever coming,
though we age and fade and die.

Music, moonlight, sighs of lovers,
help to make the world go round.
God is love, the 'Good Book' says so,
then the Dance Hall's hallowed ground.

Come the twenty-sixth September,
feet may dance, yet tears will fall.
Still that's life, it always has been,
folk, not buildings, make the ball.

S D Barr once built a ballroom,
the Flamingo brought him fame.
Gone may be, but not forgotten,
dance, youth shall, what 'er the name.

James G Kenny
Ballymena

Life Without Water

Fruitless and barren our world would be,
Void - without people like you and me,
The whole earth a desert with no waterfall,
Life without water would be no life at all.

Water is essential to keep us alive,
Without it no fish or flower can thrive,
Imagine no water to wash your face,
Just picture the plight of the whole human race.

No cattle a-lowing, no grass on the lawn,
The great ocean liners, no sea to sail on,
No boating or swimming, no wee cups of tea,
No snow on the hill slopes where folk go to ski.

So let us be thankful for clouds high and wispy,
For rain, hail and snow, and ice that is crispy,
And when the next downpour soaks to the skin,
Or the roof springs a leak - be thankful and grin.

Winnie Lees
11 November 1985
Ballybriest Cookstown

Curran

It's at a little crossroads,
in the heart of County Derry.
Famous for its duck races,
but no little folk or fairy.

Of course it must be Curran,
quite close to Tobermore.
It had a Church, school and shops,
in those days it was a goer.

The school a seat of learning,
with famous old girls and boys.
There was Boyce's shop and Toners,
who sold sweets but never toys.

The Fox and Pheasant was the pub,
folk came from far and near.
But it was bulldozed years ago,
town houses you'll find here.

There's Curran's little meeting house,
its only place of worship.
But there was Lavey & Termoneeny,
if you didn't mind the trip.

The pump sat at the centre,
and is still a focal spot.
But on so many local maps,
Curran wasn't worth a dot.

Of course time changes everything,
and that's very true of Curran.
The shops and school are closed now,
no sweets, no place to learn.

But many local names remain,
like Nelson, Hawe and Bowman.
Lennox, Kane and Duncan,
some folk don't like roamin'.

Now a local residents group,
meets in the Orange Hall.
But if that sounds one sided,
that isn't true at all.

So when you visit Mid Ulster,
to see a village still alive.
Just call at that little crossroads,
for Curran will survive.

Elizabeth Lennox
Magherafelt

Wishing My Life Away

I can't wait until tomorrow,
I wish it were next year.
I gaze into the distance,
for new horizons to appear.

I look forward to the future,
and grow older day by day.
I am so often guilty,
of wishing my life away.

If told my time was limited,
I'm sure I'd never say.
"I wish it were tomorrow",
or "there ends a dreary day".

I'd be busy for every second,
of every minute of the day.
And I'd be wishing that tomorrow,
was very far away.

So be content with life itself,
be thankful just for living.
Help others when you find you can,
and enjoy the rewards of giving.

**William Leonard
Bellaghy**

A Brilliant Man

This poem is dedicated to,
the greatest poet in the land.
No it's not Seamus Heaney,
it's another brilliant man.

Some people call him stupid,
even though that he is not.
For writing poems for charity,
with no money to be got.

He writes some poems for other men,
good poems they always are.
But at last his time has come,
for him to be the star.

No, he isn't writing this poem,
in fact it is his son.
Who would like the money to go to him,
instead of to the fund.

Daniel Leonard
Age 12
Bellaghy

Granny's The Girl

When baby arrives and around the bend drives,
new mammy and daddy who rue it.
Who can bring peace and the turmoil release,
yes, granny's the girl who can do it.

When nappy needs changed or the house rearranged,
and mammy just can't quite get through it.
There's only one thing, give the phone a wee ring,
and granny will come round and do it.

When baby played up, the noisy wee pup,
despair is how mammy will view it.
Who will come round and quieten things down,
yes, granny's the girl who can do it.

At knitting a coat for granny's wee dote,
or a wee hat and gloves to put on it.
The shops are so dear but have you no fear,
for granny's the girl who can do it.

At toddlers today where we all come to play
to clear the old mind and renew it.
If you need someone nice to offer advice,
sure granny's the girl who can do it.

Yes grannies are great at taking the weight,
when the burdens of life put you through it.
Thank her if you care for just being there,
for granny's the girl who can do it.

William Livingstone
Cullybackey

The Banks of Clady

Along the banks of Clady,
is a lovely place to dwell.
With banks and braes and bonnie glens,
it's hard to say farewell.

I remember during my childhood,
sporting through these glens.
With many lads and lasses,
I will always count as friends.

But now those days are over,
and the time is drawing near.
When I will leave this lovely spot,
the ocean wide to steer.

But I will not forget my native home,
when in a foreign land.
Nor the lovely Clady River,
that flows into the Bann.

I am going to America,
my fortune there to find.
And leave the banks of Clady,
the lads and lasses behind.

My mother told me to be wise,
and be an upright man.
And not to forget her old grey locks,
when in a foreign land.

And when I land on Columba's shore,
and meet the neighbours there.
I'll tell them of old Clady's banks,
that are so rich and fair.

I'll tell them of the corner,
that's now almost a town.
With McErlean's grand houses,
no better to be found.

I'll tell them of the factories,
and the industries that's there.
Driven by Clady River,
that gives Lagan's Mill a share.

So goodbye friends and comrades,
I am finished with my song.
I hope your prayer will be that I,
will keep away from wrong.

And when in America,
and at my daily toil.
I'll not forget old Clady's banks,
where Glenburn waters boil.

Nor my own darling sweetheart,
who is now all alone.
May God protect and guard her,
until I return home.

Henry Lynn
(1884-1955)
Clady

St Valentine's Day

Today all those who are young at heart,
will give and receive Valentines.
This old fashioned romantic custom,
has withstood the onslaught of time.

'Tis a lovely token of the deep regard,
that exists between one another,
And this ardent gesture is really a vow,
of life-long love for each other.

Unfortunately, there are those who have found,
that this fact is not always true.
For when the time of testing comes,
love fades like the morning dew.

This sign of affection is mostly observed,
by those who are still in their youth.
But for all there's a message of deeper love,
concealed in God's word of truth.

There we read of the love our Saviour bears,
for your precious soul and for mine.
'Tis beyond compare with the love declared,
in a colourful Valentine.

Human love can be warm and tender,
if perchance it is returned.
But the fervent feelings wither and die,
when that love is rejected and spurned.

Our Saviour's love for a sinful world,
true and faithful will always remain.
Altho' today many scorn that love,
and blaspheme his Holy name.

When the voice of a troubled conscience speaks,
demanding Him to depart.
Those cruel words of rejection can be,
like arrows piercing His heart.

Disappointed and grieved He may turn away,
sadly leaving you to your fate.
And some day soon when you search for Him,
you may find you are too late.

Once more the Saviour is pleading with you,
come to Him and no longer delay.
What better time to accept His love,
than on a bright St Valentine's Day.

Joyce Lynn
(1914-1997)
Ballymena

Lough Beg Shore

Some bards express in glowing words the glories of their land,
While others raise their voice and praise heroic statesmen grand
But to them I shall leave the task, let mine be to make known
The charming grace and beauties of my boyhood's happy home
Where Bann's purling waters flow 'twas there I love to stray,
Some joyous hours round sweet Lough Beg I've merrily whirled away.
I've viewed the lakes and rivers grand throughout the Emerald Isle
The Liffey, More, the Lea, the Suir, the Swilley and the Foyle,
Yet all could not compare unto the spot which I adore
Sweet place of mirth that gave me birth the Banks of Lough Beg Shore.

Oh God when I recall to mind the bliss I did enjoy,
When young and wild I blossomed forth a merry thoughtless boy
With brave friend Dick and cousin Tom and comrades many a score
Some joyful hours I merrily spent around the Annah Shore
With dog and gun around its banks my time it did employ
Or fishing with my hook and line a light gay-hearted boy
How oft' I quaffed the poteen clean with comrade full of glee
And drank success to Erin's Sons and prayed they'd soon be free
But now och home those days have gone my joyous hours are o'er
Sweet place of mirth that gave me birth the Banks of Lough Beg Shore.

How oft' I strayed with Nora dear, 'twas there I wooed and won
The fairest of the fairest fair, my own sweet Colleen bawn
When seated fondly side by side, our small boat glides along
And she cheers up my fond heart with her merry laugh and song
And many a glorious moonlight night, round Famed Church Isle I strayed
To meet the boys who feared no noise and hold our night parade
Or with our sweethearts by our sides how oft we'd merrily rove
And many a fond though flattering tale each told his lady love
Though I am doomed to leave my home I love thee more and more
Sweet place of mirth that gave me birth the Banks of Lough Beg Shore.

Alas unto some distant clime my course I now must steer
Yes fate decrees that I must part with all that life holds dear
The charming maids and dashing blades so loving and so kind
With school mates gay and comrades free I must leave all behind
Fair well brave old friends of mine I'll ever think of you
Oh Nora dear pride of this heart must I leave thee too
I'll seek a home where freedom shines beyond the surging wave
In that fair land the exiles home sweet refuge of the brave
I'll yet return to thee I trust with wealth and fame galore
Sweet place of mirth that gave me birth the Banks of Lough Beg Shore.

Michael Lynn
(1860-1941)
Portglenone/New Zealand

Mullaghnamoyagh Hill

Down in the Bann's sweet valley,
and looking west you'll see
A hill from out of the boglands rise,
a hill that is dear to me.

For many a time its sides I climbed,
in youth with a right good will
And many a happy hour I spent,
on Mullaghnamoyagh Hill.

Its top is crowned with heather,
It's not a mountain bare
And many a cottage round its base,
nestles snugly there.

In ancient times the old folk tell,
and they cross themselves from ill
The Druids lit their Beltean fires,
on Mullaghnamoyagh Hill.

And from that time until this day,
as mid summer night comes around
A bonfire blazed as sure as fate,
with many a merry sound.

And boys and girls met round the blaze,
and talked of love until
T'was time to say the Rosary,
on Mullaghnamoyagh Hill.

Eastwards stands the Antrim hills,
to the river sloping down
And in the distance can be seen,
the Mourne Mountains brown.

Sleive Gallion rears her lofty crest,
and further westward still
The gallant Cairntougher smiles,
on Mullaghnamoyagh Hill.

Northwards the Clady river runs,
along it's stony bed
And just across is old Greenlough,
where sleeps our sainted dead.

And where we hope ourselves to sleep,
in blessed peace until
The sound of Michael's trumpet breaks,
over Mullaghnamoyagh Hill.

John T Marron
(1921-1998)
Clady/USA

The Lad

They were no great aff-set anywhere,
the scutchers times ago.
For drink it folly'd the most of them,
that wrought among the tow.

Plenishment they'd have little or noan,
except for what they'd stale.
An' they'd make the childer go out an' beg,
gowpins of oaten male.

I knowed a scutcher that wrought in Shane,
he was a drunken scrub.
But he reared a son, an' I mind the son,
a smart wee lump of a cub.

His clo'es were wings, an' his cap was tore,
an' his fire was the fire at the kill.
An' he went to school on his wee bare feet,
an' niver got half his fill.

Above the mill was a quare big hill,
he could see the graveyard wall.
To the market-house, an' the station gates,
an' the new Hibernian Hall.

You'd hear him singin' goan up the hill,
but the dear knows why he sung.
For the people thought they would see the day,
when his da would sure be hung.

When the Twelfth was near he'd march the road,
his drumsticks in his han',
Boys, he was prime at the double rowl,
on the lid of an oul tin can.

He played his lone, for the other folk,
were ashamed of him an' his rags.
So he thrinneld his hoop an' waded the burn,
an' ginneld for spricklybags.

I mind the year he took up with me,
the ploughin' had just begun.
I'd watch him leadin' the horses roun',
the drunken scutcher's son.

Little I thought that afterwards,
more than a son he'd be.
For his father died in a water-shough,
an' he come to live with me.

He was odd in a way, I think he heered,
what nobody else could hear.
An' he seen what I could never see,
the more my sight was clear.

The top of a hill bewitched him still,
an' the flame at the mountain's rim,
But a runnin' burn was the best of all,
for he sayed it sung till him.

There were some that went that far as to say,
he was sure to turn out wil'.
But the wee lad grew till he grew man big,
an' kept the heart of a chile.

The longer he lived about the place,
the less I had to fear.
There was never a word from him to me,
but done me good to hear.

I'm feelin' oul' since he went away,
an' my sight is gettin' dim.
I niver axed for to keep him back,
when they needed men like him.

He's sleepin' now where the poppies grow,
in the coat that bullets tore.
An' what's a wheen of medals to me,
when my own wee lad's no more.

W F Marshall
(1888-1959)
Sixmilecross

Keady's Side

Where Cairn Burn loiters,
and shinney waters flow.
Down to Aghadowey,
in the vale below.

This is poet's country,
whatever else betide.
As towering high to heaven,
shines old Keady's side.

Other hills are higher,
and of deeper blue.
But their face is my questionnaire,
and weather forecast too.

When the rain clouds gather,
we put an inch to our stride.
As on the wings of the wind,
it spreads from Keady's side.

But when the sky is cloudless,
and deep the blue behind.
I'll lift my old two wheeler,
and leave my coat behind.

A little mirth, a little faith,
a touch of sadness too.
The gentle calm of healing sleep,
will see the long day through.

And in the coming morning,
with hope we'll step outside.
To see the new light and shadow,
upon old Keady's side.

Many generations who have seen thee,
have passed to their reward.
As per chance full soon will happen,
to your contemporary bard.

But while there's time let me thank God,
for the memories of beauties that abide.
A pool of light, a splash of dark,
a plume of smoke upon the Keady's side.

Liam McAllister
(1899-1975)
Aghadowey

The Moneysharvin Girls

The girls I see in sweet Tirhugh,
and some in Swatragh too.
And old fair maids in old Gortade,
and some in Culnagrew.
And I am sure that Gortinure,
must have some, less or more.
There were girls there you could love one time,
way back in eighty four.

Slaghtneil, Tirkane, also Halfgayne,
you'll meet them in their crowds.
All highly educated,
but perhaps a trifle proud.
The Macknagh girls are straight and tall,
sedate and all serene.
But you go to Moneysharvin,
for the making of a queen.

You can see them there with auburn hair,
or hair of lighter hue.
Or hair that's like the raven's wing,
they have me raving too.
With skirts cut wide their charms to hide,
swing well below the knee.
You would praise the Lord to have your sight,
their beauty for to see.

On Sunday morning when they pass,
to go and say their prayers.
Their footsteps wouldn't bend the grass,
they fairly walk on air.
They fast and pray both night and day,
to gain the cron of stars.
But I wouldn't wish them angels,
they're much better as they are.

So now dear girls, God bless your curls,
I've made this all too long.
I can thrash or dig or mow a rig,
but I cannot make a song.
But while I've strength to raise my voice,
twill be my earnest prayer.
Good luck to Moneysharvin girls,
and ribbons for their hair.

Mick McAtamney
(1860-1946)
Swatragh

Bann Water

(On her return from a walk along the Bann, I asked my
granddaughter, then aged 4, what colour the water was.)

"It's black," she said, with infant emphasis.

Not Blue, when white swans rested silent,
And willows drooped to comb its rippling locks;
Nor sunned, with mirrored buttercups,
As children sought for biting trout;
Nor pale, as dun cows blinked
At scampering minnows;
Nor pied, when soft Cistercian chants
Exorcised the waiting water,
Blessing quick and dead
And sweet'ning acid history.

"Black," she said, "Granda, it's black."

To her it had revealed
Its yearly toll of corpses;
Old sunken Norse in pillage-laden craft;
Invaders' spirits jellied in darkness;
Souls in suicide-dammed,
Dubious, eternal peace.

"I saw it, and it's black," said tiny Maebh.

Matt McAteer
Portglenone

A Season Turning

Along the Bann's late summer banks,
the evening lays long shadows.
As we strike out upon a walk,
to Richard's lower meadow.

There once, beneath a benweed root,
I found a wriggling worm.
And tied it to a line and hook,
to lure a silver salmon.

For to the benweed's golden crown,
the butterflies will come.
To lay their eggs and at its' roots,
you'll always find their young.

The rowan, red, is on our path,
sweet smells the meadowsweet.
An early tint is in the bough,
and lately swallows meet.

A buzzard soars on widespread wings,
surveying in the valley.
His purple heather-bell and ling,
his myrtle, birch and sally.

And fruitless from frostbitten blooms,
here stands a barren thorn.
And clustered nuts, abundantly,
these hazel trees adorn.

Then venturing in the gathering dusk,
their sightless flights to follow.
The bats steal out and echoes of,
long voices fade before us.

W J McCann
27 August 1998
Portglenone

71

Parents

What do you think when we worry and fuss,
what are you thinking of parents like us.
Can you guess at our fears when we see you go out,
do you even know what life is about.

Do you know of the dangers that stand in your way,
when you're tempted by life, will you stand up and say.
No I really won't do it, I won't go along,
my parents have taught me to know right from wrong.

Do you know of our joy when you were first born,
can you guess at our pride when we held your small form.
But time hurried by and you soon learned to walk,
it seemed no time at all before you could talk.

We worried and fretted when you were in pain,
and prayed oh so hard for your smile once again.
May some of the knowledge we've tried to impart,
and some of the love that we feel in our heart.

Help you to pick out the path you must take,
and act as a guide in decisions you make.
For all we can do now your childhood has flown,
is to stand by and watch you step out on your own.

For we know when you hold a new life in your hands,
only then comes the moment when you'll understand.
All the reasons behind all the worry and fuss,
for that is the day you'll be parents like us.

Andy McClean
(1907-1981)
Glengormley 1940

72

The Banks of The River Maine

My thoughts in fancy take their flight,
To days when just a boy.
Where carelessly I wandered through,
The green fields around Dunloy.
I've seen great lands and mansions grand,
And cities of great fame.
But no finer spot than my humble cot,
On the banks of the River Maine.

God bless the place where I was born,
A heaven on this earth to me.
Though sadly from where I was torn,
To look for work, it had to be.
I would seek my fame and fortune there,
And come back once again.
To my home in Dunloy, where I played as a boy,
On the banks of the sweet River Maine.

I've seen that far off fields look green,
And the girls there are pretty and fair.
But I really do mean that none I have seen,
With the girls of Dunloy can compare.
Good health on my travels I seemed to enjoy,
But my fortune I did not obtain.
I came back much wiser to my home in Dunloy,
On the banks of the sweet River Maine.

Jim McClements
Dunloy

The Ould Rocking Chair

Clickety click goes my ould rocking chair,
The warm summer breeze stirs my snow-white hair.
I'm thinking of days when my body was strong,
And my voice could be heard in a good lively song.
All that is gone now, but I won't complain,
Close my eyes and take refuge in memories again.

My vision is clear and my mind flies with joy,
To the time of my youth as a bare-footed boy,
Each day was perfection, be it wet or fine,
Life was for living, no thought of decline.
Active and eager, no pain, no regret,
The world was my oyster, unopened yet.

My TV was large, they're made smaller now,
My chair hard and high, on a tree's leafy bough,
The country my screen, from sky to the ground,
To watch other 'channels' I just turned around.
TV time I had none, no aerial, no coil,
No bursting valve, no electric fault, could my viewing spoil.

No velvet-tongued announcer was needed to convey
The song of lark or cuckoo, the smell of new-mown hay,
The sound of scythe or sickle, cutting golden corn,
Or the bellow of an anxious cow for her calf just newly born.
Tuneful thrushes, buzzing bees, continuous music played,
Viewing lasted dawn to dusk, no licence fee was paid.

I knew where birds nested and where, in the Spring,
Wild flowers would blossom and beauty would bring,
I knew them by name, where each clump could be got,
Every year I'd bring home some to grow in a pot.
How I loved the wee forest, its green sward to tread,
Or watch the blue skies through the trees overhead.

The schoolhouse had one room, in winter a fire
Kept us warm, while from old Mr Tait we'd enquire,
Why Sir, and how Sir, and when, which and whether,
Though he explained well I was still in a dither.
I'd no head for books, figures drove me to tears,
I regretted this sadly in after school years.

As I grew to manhood, my learning was sound,
At all local markets I was known and renowned
As a man who knew trading, decent and square,
New Year till December I ne'er missed a fair.
Now they've co-op'd the markets, you get a cheque by post,
No money changed, no dealer's punt, the fair day's just a ghost.

I wooed young Annie Mullan, a blithesome lass was she,
With long black hair, deep blue eyes, she turned the heart in me,
When she agreed to marry me, my joy could not be told,
We both went out next market day and bought a ring of gold.
We set a date for early Spring, but God took the life he gave,
And on Patrick's Day I placed the ring on darling Annie's grave.

I never could forget her, no other girl did wed,
So, for forty lonely years, a bachelor's life I've lead,
A good life, an honest life, I've worked with crop and sod,
And I know I'll meet my Annie, when I hear the call of God.
My weary bones are waiting Him to give my day an end,
Till then my book of memories is this old man's best friend.

Sally McCorry
April 1967
Bellaghy

The Old School In Gortgole

I'm thinking tonight of the days long ago,
As an old fashioned picture I see
It brings back fond memories of days that are gone,
Of the days that are dearest to me.
Down memory's lane, let my thoughts wander back,
To be "present" again on the roll,
And infancy again there to answer my name,
At that old fashioned school in Gortgole.

The years have rolled by since I sat there to pose,
For that picture my eyes now behold.
And thanks to a lady who treasured with care.
A gem that's more precious than gold.
No tinsel or show as I gaze on each row,
Not the slightest attempt to cajole.
As we sat side by side, we can look back with pride.
To that old-fashioned school in Gortgole.

How little we thought of the battles ahead,
In the hard world of struggle and strife,
The ups and the downs, the smiles and the frowns,
On the troublesome pathway of life.
Some have been destined to travel afar,
Though oceans between surge and roll,
Their thoughts fondly go back to youth's happy day,
At that old-fashioned school in Gortgole.

Those walls that once glistened in ivory white
Are now crumbling fast to decay.
The glories that shone in the dear distant past
Are almost forgotten today.
Though weeds now abound in profusion around,
In the spot which my praises extol,
Down memory's lane I'll wander again,
To that old-fashioned school in Gortgole.

Pat McGroggan
(1898-1957)
Portglenone

The Old School Days

That road has never changed much,
the scene is just the same.
I sauntered up it ten long years,
through sunshine snow and rain.

'Tis many a weary day I spent,
although against the rule.
As I thought the time would never come,
when I'd depart from Floughy school.

Those five hours we spent in it,
for five days in the week.
It was paradise when you think of it,
if the truth you will only speak.

There was many a thought went o'er our mind,
as the hand began to smart.
And as soon as the clock hit three o'clock,
for the door we made a dart.

We were all one big family,
we learned the golden rule.
As we sat with troubled faces,
in gloomy Floughy school.

But time rolled on and came the day,
when happy there I sat.
For once outside at three o'clock,
I'd no more cross the mat.

But never wish the time away,
or you will be a fool.
For I'm thinking of those happy days,
in gloomy Floughy School.

Bobby McGuiggan
Randalstown

The Old Home Town

It's hard to live on these Prairies Dave,
With its terrible frost and snow,
And it's mighty hard to stick it out
Where the Northern Blizzards blow.

But the old blood still is in me
And I laugh at the Blizzards frown,
For I'm a County Derry man
From old Bellaghy Town.

Oh, it's old Bellaghy Town Dave,
Of its scenes I love to tell,
Palmers Hill, The Shilling Hill
And its famous Jean Bell's Well.

The Barrack hall and old Stair Head
To memory I recall,
King William Street I'll ne'er forget,
Nor the dear old Orange Hall.

There were McIntyres and Martins,
Millikens and Brown,
Mawhinneys and McMurdies
Always at their post were found,

Porters too from Old Drumlamph
And the loyal Bruces' too,
The loyal Blairs from Mullaghboy
And those Kennedy lads so true.

Oh I know I would die happy Dave,
If I once more could roam,
Through those lovely scenes and valley green
Where once we called our home.

To stand once more by the old Orange Hall,
It would fill my heart with joy
To live those old times over again
Like when you and I were Boys.

Dave McMurdie
(1868-1960)
Bellaghy/Canada

70th Birthday

Threads of gold and some of black,
are weaving to and fro.
To take us on a journey,
started 70 years ago.

The picture that's emerging,
is one of joy and tears.
But most of all it's showing,
70 ful-filling years.

And as we watch the sunsset,
across the canvas spread.
All of the darkest images,
are edged with golden thread.

The man that's here appearing,
has a proud ambitious mind.
He knows his many talents,
were his to help mankind.

So here we are with pleasure,
on this memorable night.
To join in celebration,
with the man who got it right.

Mary McPoland
Dunloy

The River Bann

First of all the rivers
Childhood's eyes could see;
Now in years maturer,
Rest my eyes on thee.

Mourne with many streamlets
Gives to thee a start;
Ulster river passing,
Factory and mart.

Banbridge and Gilford both
Only thy banks are placed;
Boats and rowers also
On thy waters traced.

Happy-hearted workers
Gaze upon thy wave;
From the fields and meadows
Which thy currents lave.

Sun and shadow mingle,
On thy waters blent;
But the Bann keeps flowing
On her mission bent.

Wending, wending slowly
From the heart of Down;
Passing in thy journey
Busy Portadown.

Flowing, flowing into
Bosom of Lough Neagh;
But her fond caresses
Do not make thee stay.

Toome with all her people
See thee gliding down;
With a bow most gracious
To their border town.

Just a passing tribute
To our own Lough Beg;
But thy motto ever
Duty must not flag.

History round thee gathers
Memory o'er me steals;
Thou hast seen the goings
Of the famed O'Neills.

But thy work un-ended
Hardy fisher son;
Portglenone and Kilrea
See thee flowing on.

For thy salmon glorious
Well-esteemed and more;
Anglers read the story
In their fishing lore.

Sunbeams kiss thy dimples
Winds may make thee roar;
But thou flowest onward,
There is work in store.

Flowing on and onward
Through the gleams of rain;
Till thou touch in passing
Town of sweet Coleraine.

Where the broad Atlantic
Clasps to mother heart;
Gentle, glorious river,
Thou hast done thy part.

David Gordon Montgomery
(1860-1953)
February 1934
Portglenone

Memory

Oh joyful thing is memory,
in an instant I recall.
Those happy carefree childhood days,
the sweetest days of all.

Oh wondrous thing is memory,
to bring again so near.
The friends who have gone on before,
those whom we hold so dear.

Oh useful thing is memory,
a store of all my ken.
And when I need a piece of it,
I call it back again.

Oh fearful thing is memory,
wounds to the flesh soon heal.
But hurts stored up in the memory,
such pain and grief conceal.

Oh mystic thing is memory,
no science yet explains.
How we perceive so many things,
and store them in our brains.

Without the use of memory,
I'd have no place called home.
I wouldn't know my dearest friends,
I would be all alone.

R J Mowbray
Magherafelt

Boundary Stream

Where the two counties meet and the clear water flow
Along Lissan River I often times go.
To stroll by the stream as it rambles its way,
From the hills around Lissan to the shores of Lough Neagh.

This river is rough and it's many miles long
And it sure served the needs of the folk that are gone.
Back in the days when the carries are filled
And people made use of the old water mills.

Flow on lovely river flow gently along,
While the birds in the bushes will sing their sweet song.
And I will continue to ramble and stray,
By the boundary stream that flows down to Lough Neagh.

It's grand to be here on a long day in spring
And perhaps hear the bells of the local churches ring.
Or gaze from the fort away up on the hill
And see the remains of the Lissan sawmill.

With a rod and a line here contented you'd be
Catching the wee fish coming up from the sea.
And maybe get one that would do for the tay
From the boundary stream that flows down to Lough Neagh.

The sun is going down and it's now getting late
And I have arrived at the Lissan sluice gate.
Where the water is gauged the light for to make
And the clock on the castle has just now struck eight.
So I take my leave now and go on my way
From the boundary stream that flows down to Lough Neagh.

Daniel Neeson
Cookstown

The Blacksmith

I'm a hardworking blacksmith, my name is Dan Kerr,
and the sound of my anvil can be heard near and far.
What I have done lately has caused me to wail,
I gave up my good trade and I started to deal.

It was on Thursday morning, I mind well the day,
when to Magherafelt I did straight take my way.
As I jogged along I did whistle and sing,
and the first place I landed was Tom Larkin's ring.

There were all kinds of animals, it looked like a show,
there were cows, pigs and horses and donkeys also.
The horses came first in the programme of sale,
I said I would buy one, if I could get bail.

When I finished dealing it was long after night,
and I landed home with a chap called Joe Wright.
I awoke the next morning and I looked at my squad,
the old horse in particular, I nearly went mad.

I tore at my hair, round the house I did roam,
I got Susie and Joe to take the horse home.
Back landed Susie and Joe with the horse,
they landed at Larkin's and asked for the boss.

Old Larkin came out with a face like a Turk,
"I'll not take him back, there's no fault in his work.
I don't give a damn should he feed him on whey,
Dan Kerr has him now and he'll have him to pay."

Hugh O'Connor
(1912-1998)
The Grange Desertmartin

The Braidwater Mill

I crave your kind attention,
and I hope a page to fill.
Concerning the Braidwater,
the local spinning mill.

It stands beside the River Braid,
it stands there so serene.
A monument to greater days,
that long ago have been.

It's silent now, in distant time,
its work has ceased alas.
But it lives on in the hearts of those,
who knew its glorious past.

It was famous for flax spinning yarn,
o'er a hundred years or so.
And from this top class product,
all our linen goods would flow.

Its workers came from every part,
of town and countryside.
Its name became a household word,
and was known far and wide.

And the workers from the villages,
of Ahoghill and Broughshane.
Often walked to the Braidwater Mill,
in winter's snow and rain.

Workers came from Harryville,
and from Pennybridge as well.
From Ballymarlow and Liminary,
their endeavours too I tell.

There were also the "halftimers",
(call them what you will).
Who spent half the week at lessons,
the rest inside the Mill.

The children had to work then,
to earn a little pay.
There were no special benefits,
so you could live the easy way.

The people who were taken on,
had various jobs to fill.
They all had special work to do,
at the Braidwater Spinning Mill.

I'll not forget the office staff,
the managers as well.
Spinning masters and overlookers,
their contributions tell.

Without the guidance of the men,
who key positions fill.
We never would have known the name,
the great Braidwater Mill.

I salute you now Braidwater,
and the workers of your day.
You laid the firm foundations,
of our prosperous town today.

By giving constant employment,
throughout your glorious reign.
You helped the families of your day,
and the town which bears your name.

So good luck to all past workers,
you are well remembered still.
For your hard work and endeavour,
in the historic Braidwater Mill.

Tommy O'Hara
(1908-1999)
Ballymena

The Mayogall Donkeys

You have heard about the camels in the Asiatic lan',
how they carry heavy burdens o'er the red and burnin' san'.
You have heard about the asses in the ancient days of Saul,
but you've maybe never l'arnt how they came to Mayogall.

An' they're there, I will swear, as they were among the Jews,
some respected, some neglected, some unshod an' some with shoes.
They're very useful animals, an' when they're dead, they say,
their skins are fashioned into drums for use on Patrick's day.

Well, in Fox's "Book of Martyrs" it does carefully explain,
that when Saul had lost his asses he came quickly home again.
Ab' informed his aged father that a man whose name was Paul,
had skidaddled with the donkeys an' was boun' for Mayogall.

He went trampin' an' stampin' across the German plain,
he welted an' pelted all down through France an' Spain.
Inquirin' of the peasantry who lived in ancient Gaul,
if they could point him out the road that led to Mayogall.

One day I saw a cavalcade of donkeys slowly driven,
'twas boun' with loads of cabbage plants, for parts beyon' Dungiven.
All ages an' all pedigrees, all marshalled in a line,
I counted them both large an' small, they numbered twenty nine.

When they brayed, sure, they made such a tremendous soun',
you'd have swore that the roar would have opened up the groun'.
It was taken up in chorus by donkeys of Drumard,
an' was answered back like thunder from their brethren in Killard.

Now among them was an oul' one with a coat of lightish brown,
he reached the top ot Tamsey's Hill an' after that lay down.
His master in distraction to him did loudly say,
"by actin' thus our merchandise will not get soul' the day.

91

So, get up or the whip I'll be usin', right or wrong,
do your best like the rest for I know you're quite as strong.
The donkey, makin' answer, said, "you shouldn't me abuse,
for twenty miles is rather far to travel without shoes".

"In Ballymacpeake," his master said, "they never wear a shoe,
an' roun' the hills of Kernaman they're just the same as you.
The worthy folk of Granaghan have always thought it right,
to keep their donkeys barefoot to pillage in the night."

I was young, I was strong, I was twice the age of you,
a courtin' an' sportin, with neither sock nor shoe.
Attended wakes an' dances all over the oul' sod,
an' I made my first proposal on the day I first got shod.

So, get up, my lad, an' shake yourself, an' do your level best,
an' when we reach Pat Bradley's we'll stop an' take a rest.
We're sure to sell the load of greens 'twixt here an' Maghera,
an' after that you'll only have the cart an' me to dhra'.

O' I know where to go when I want to sell the greens,
there's the Boyles an' Coyles an' the Bradleys an' the Breens.
An' roun' by Cluntygera, sure, they think them quite a feast,
tho' they give them indigestion an' they have to call the priest."

The donkey bounded to his feet an' gave a wicked pull,
an' soon they got to Bradleys, an' there they both got full.
Pat bought the greens an' donkey for a shillin' an' a glass,
a price that brought a protest from the self-respectin' ass.

How he roared an' bellored beats the power of my pen,
an' such an awful consternation did he cause throughout the glen.
That they bought a ton of dynamite an' swore, both one an' all,
that they'd blow the ass to Jericho, Belfast or Mayogall.

James O'Kane
(1832-1913)
Swatragh

A Helping Hand

Ah, boys and girls give an ear to me,
and hear now what I say.
Enjoy your youth and happy be,
do a good deed every day.

There will be times when you are feeling low,
and you think you can't go on.
Get up and go, let that spirit rise,
it's just the dark before the dawn.

As you travel on that road through life,
there will be hills and braes.
But carry on, reach out your hand,
help those in borrowed days.

If this you do then go that mile,
and a good Samaritan be.
Always give your hand to those that fall,
and those that cannot see.

The future it is in your hands,
be honest kind and true.
These virtues mind, as you go through time,
then your sins they will be few.

Keep clear your mind, have no ill thoughts,
and always walk the line.
If this you do where 'ere' you go,
God's richest gift be thine.

Norman Porter
8 December 2002
Toomebridge

Jean Bell's Well

Thy poets oft have sung of wine -
Indeed they should be tired
Since Bacchus first in mystic days
Their harps and song inspired.

But muse of mine has soberer theme,
And just delights to tell,
In accents rustic as itself,
Of dear old Jean Bell's well.

Ah! Days of childhood come to me
With all your fairy train,
Speak to my heart and waken there
Your memories again.

Dress in their summer best the fields,
And don't forget the dell
Where just beneath the Shillin Hill
Sits placid Jean Bell's well.

I see again the meadows green
Where for a live-long day
The sun-god touched with richer gold
The yellow flowers of May.

I hear again the gurgling stream
Where shade of willow fell
Beside the crystal water sounds
Of ancient Jean Bell's well.

I hear the children's voices rise
To meet the larks on high.
As he pours forth his evening hymn
From out the sunset sky.

The children then - where are they now?
For some has rung the knell.
And some have crossed the sea, and some
Still drink at Jean Bell's well.

There is the mill, it's wheel at rest,
And there the Castle wall.
From 'mong it's trees the old church spire
Points stately, grey and tall.

And there the peaceful village lies
Girt round by field and fell
I see them as I sit and muse
Beside Dear Jean Bell's well.

Why do these lifeless things remain?
Why do our loved ones go?
Why do I hear in song's refrain
Voices of long ago?

I ask while dreaming of the past,
And shrink from the potent spell,
Of thoughts that come from far away
By silent Jean Bell's well.

Youth will pass, and the world is wide
And far-off fields are green.
And young hearts turn so eagerly
To paths untried, unseen.

But give me the quiet ways of life
And let me ever dwell,
'Mid scenes that flourished long ago
Around old Jean Bell's well.

Then in my dreams the silent past
Will e'er come back to me.
I shall bear again the voices call
Over life's shadowed sea.

The friends of youth will roam once more
In meadow and in dell.
And life will be a summer time
By long-loved Jean Bell's well.

James Patton Spence
(1862-1936)
Bellaghy

Forty Who's Countin'

Well I'm goin' tae be forty the morrow,
and sure forty is not all that oul.
But ye hear some brat callin' ye an oul doll,
and ye feel ye could knock him out coul'.

But when ye have time tae think o'er it,
ye can mind what you thought of it still.
That most folk were past it at thirty,
and at forty they were over the hill.

Now it always has been my ambition,
tae reach forty without a grey hair.
So if one comes to my attention,
I'd make sure it did not stay long there.

But I'll relax after the morrow,
and let myself grow old with grace.
For you always know ones that's been tintin',
it just doesn't match their oul' face.

And Lord, not another wee wrinkle,
I never saw that one before.
So I'll buy some of that Oil of Ulay,
and hope it prevents any more.

Some people say, don't call them wrinkles,
it's nicer to say laughter lines.
If that was what done it, I'm tellin' ye,
I must have had some quare laughs in me time.

Ye might catch a glimpse of your reflection,
in them shop mirrors as ye go through.
And for a second it just doesn't hit ye,
that thon middle aged woman, is you.

Ye run into some childhood acquaintance,
she may be dressed up in jewels and fir.
But ye spot the grey hairs and you're thinkin'
boys, I'm stickin' it better than her.

While you're sayin' hello, and how are ye,
and she's sayin' somethin' the same.
Ye're racking yer brains, but it's useless,
for ye just can't remember her name.

And as ye retreat in confusion,
ye start thinkin', me memory's gone.
Is this the onset of me dotage,
now there's something to ponder upon.

The weans think I'm just an oul fogey,
they won't wear one thing that I choose.
Their eyes open wide in pure horror,
sayin', I wouldn't be seen dead in them shoes.

But some people hold other opinions,
they say your life's only begun.
When ye reach that 4.0., you should venture,
to find your own place in the sun.

But, the back's a bit dodgy, the eyes a bit dim,
and of youth I have not found the fountain.
So tomorrow they'll say, are ye forty today,
I'll say, aye, I'm just forty, whose countin'.

Maud Steele
Kilrea

Bonnie Ahoghill

I hope in these lines you will all understand,
this graphic description of facts at her hand.
Concerning Ahoghill, our birthplace and home,
though seldom it's mentioned in verse or a poem.

We're proud of our village, so ancient and fair,
and oft-times we've heard many old folk declare.
Before Ballymena was given its name,
we existed in strength o'er the banks of the Maine.

We have eight grocers' stores, aye and three pubs forby,
so we eat when we're hungry and drink when we're dry.
Fresh butter and milk, from the creamery at hand,
we enjoy our "small ration" of Ivy Leaf Brand.

We have two sturdy blacksmiths and a neat cobblers shop,
we've a new police barracks with a fine range of cops.
And the local spud merchant, his days work begun,
can supply your demands from a stone to a ton.

There's the wee sub post-office with its red painted sign,
where the name of our village is boldly outlined.
On Fridays' they're busy with pensioners' claims,
while on Tuesdays' they'll pay you eight bob for the "weans".

I could mention lots more, but I haven't the time,
so I hope you've enjoyed every verse, every line.
And as said by the traveller who stopped to survey,
it's the finest wee town in auld Ireland today.

Bobby Stewart
(1910-1976)
Ahoghill

The Homes Of Moneyglass

O, all the world's a like to me,
and natures beauties rare.
An' trees or flower or verdant vale,
are pleasant everywhere.
But yet no sunny land on earth,
for me can e'er surpass.
The quiet hills and rippling rills,
and homes of Moneyglass.

And those like me, whose lives were spent,
amid those happy dells.
And every stile and ivied wall,
a fond remembrance tells.
Ah, how they trace each curving road,
each winding lane and pass.
To the little whitewashed chapel,
'mid the homes of Moneyglass.

O memories of those early years,
when as a boy I trod.
To the modest church beside the grove,
to know and learn of God.
And the good priest smiled with tender care,
on the happy children's class.
In the little whitewashed chapel,
'mid the homes of Moneyglass.

And sure as Sunday morning came,
we all were gathered there.
When Holy Mass was offered up,
the young, the old, the fair.
And when the Sursum Corda road,
in tones we loved so well.
We lifted up our hearts in praise,
at the tinkling of a bell.

In praise to God for gifts to all,
no thought or rank or class.
In that little whitewashed chapel,
'mid the homes of Moneyglass.
And O' our faith has flourished,
still with the passing years.
And now beside the tottering church,
a beauteous House appears.

With tall spire lifted up to heaven,
where once there grew a sod.
A zealous plaster's crowning work,
for his people and for God.
To proudly tell to all who seek,
as years may come to pass.
That Irelands faith still brightly shines,
'mid the homes of Moneyglass.

Owen Toal
(1869-1949)
Toomebridge

Winter Friend

There's a robin on my windowsill,
with breast so bright and red.
And I know he's waiting patiently,
for me to get him fed.

And how could I refuse him,
for when it comes to spring.
And I'm digging in the garden,
then he's sure to come and sing.

When March winds still are blowing,
there will be no time to rest.
For together with his little mate,
they'll build a cosy nest.

Were you to ask a builder,
be he best in all the land.
He could build no finer dwelling,
from a specimen or plan.

Robins know it's so important,
that they find a site that's right.
Safe away from predators,
and cold winds' frosty bite.

Now I've fed you, little robin,
but I know it won't be long.
Until you return my kindness,
with your chirpy little song.

Doreen E Todd
Portglenone

My Helicopter

I have a bold ambition,
fantastic it may seem.
To own a helicopter,
'tis not an idle dream.

'Twould be a welcome asset,
save energy and time.
An exalted type of transit,
in keeping with the times.

I'll shop around a bit,
and view what models be.
But in the end if possible,
a mini sure for me.

I'm in a choice environ,
have a plot of ground.
Will suit a canny lift off,
and a gentle touch down.

I'd hop to church on Sunday,
drop down on the car park.
Would cause a sensation,
if only for the lark.

I'd duly inform our P.P.,
he might rightly object.
Even my overtures,
he could flatly reject.

I may be pessimistic,
but don't deny the trait.
For the finis on this venture,
I can only speculate.

Adversity calls with most,
my plans may be negative.
But with perseverance,
can see an alternative.

I'll visit the monastery,
and explain to the Abbot alone.
There is ample accommodation,
near the town of Portglenone.

I have joined an aeriel club,
an doing my best.
If progress continues,
soon I'll stand my test.

But am deeply involved,
for one in my situation.
With purchase tax soaring,
all blamed on inflation.

But I hope to carry on,
listen to the instructor.
Hope to roar overhead,
in my helicopter.

E J Toner
(1909-1987)
Bellaghy
December 1983

Magherafelt Court

Folk fritter a fortune
and pay through the nose,
for concerts and circuses
and cinema shows.

Unconscious that heaps
of full free gratis sport,
is provided each quarter
in Magherafelt Court.

There is tragedy rarely
and drama galore,
laughter and merriment,
jokes by the score.

Few casual performers
appear on that stage,
but a good old stock company,
seasoned and sage.

Yonder McGuckian,
who's father we knew,
Henry and Hastings,
Malone and Agnew.

Well they get started at length
and the Registrar groans,
as the oath is repeated
in mumbling tones.

Some still kiss the book
with a sibbering suck,
and hold up the right hand
at the same time for luck.

"Would you just tell Your Honour
and please turn about,
if deceased died intestate
and kindly speak out".

The witness looks daggers
and tosses her head,
"he died in no testate,
he died in his bed.

And my sister's girl Lizzie,
that married McPake,
made the boulster and sheets
and all for the wake".

Though a nicer ould corpse,
(here I pause to report),
and the scribes in their shorthand
wrote, "Laughter in Court".

But the witness continues
in accent more shrill,
till His Honour speaks out,
"did your man make a will".

"Well it's this way Your Honour,
my Uncle Pat's Mick,
went away to New Zealand
the year he took sick.

We were watching a sow
we expected to pig",
and His Honour exploded
and shifted his wig.

The court titters with laughter
and the Registrar rocks,
"for heaven's sake woman
get down from the box.

For we would need suction pumps
to get evidence out,
of a witness like this,
who is hedging no doubt".

Well the next case was slander,
and language obscene,
and the witness swore,
there was wigs on the green.

And defendants seduced them
and slandered them sore,
and went back generations
into family lore.

Defendants denied this
and turned up their eyes,
and dismissed the whole thing
as a bundle of lies.

"And for her", cries the female
defendant with scorn,
"that's the damdest ould villan
that ever was born.

And her father before her,
the neighbours all knew,
was the greatest ould rogue
from the Bann to the Roe".

And the witness continues
and shaking his fist,
till His Honour cries "Halt!
the case is dismissed".

Well the sessions continues
from day on to day,
with slander and warranty,
wills, right of way.

They question, cross question,
they lie and they swear,
over some insignificant
sordid affair.

Their potatoes are still
to be dug if you look,
and the hay's in the hand cock
and the corn's in the stook.

And they are suing for sixpence
and spending a pound,
but be sure that's the way
that money goes round.

And the lawyers get wealthy
and the client's get lean,
and His Honour develops
a penchant spleen.

Louis J Walsh
(1880-1942)
Maghera/Letterkenny

Nostalga

How often as I linger,
in the cool of the evening air.
I think of my native country,
and my loved ones dwelling there.

The sunset of whose beauty,
poets wrote and loved to see.
The golden sands deserted,
the smell of peat, beside the lea.

To hear the music of the lark,
the accents sweet and low.
Of country folk and simple tastes,
and loving hearts that show.

A welcome to each stranger there,
whoever he may be.
How oft I wish when memories stir,
that it could be for me.

Anna M Ward (née Dale)
Randalstown/England

Someone Is Waiting

Far away there's someone waiting,
for a foot that never falls.
Far away there's someone listening,
for a voice that never calls.

It may be the golden summer,
it may be the winter time.
Springtime, Summer, Autumn, Winter,
someone thinks of you tonight.

Write a letter home to mother,
send your love to dear old dad.
Tell them that you're well and happy,
though perhaps you're feeling sad.

Never tell the world your troubles,
smiles are better far than tears.
Tell them that you're coming home soon,
though it may not be for years.

Far away a sprig of ivy,
clings around a cabin door.
Far away a robin red-breast,
sings its sweet love-song of yore.

Far away a light is burning,
in yon window clear and bright.
Far away you're not forgotten,
someone thinks of you tonight.

Author unknown

Tragedy

Robert Reid and Agnes Henry,
names we never shall forget.
For their tragic fate shall linger,
oh the fateful day they met.

Met by Clady's flowing waters,
on that dark November night.
In the twinkling of a moment,
never more to see the light.

Sudden death! a death from drowning,
one brief struggle for the bank.
Sinking, fighting, deeper, deeper,
one last gasp and then they sank.

Now their bodies are recovered,
friends and strangers gather round.
On the features of beholders,
sympathy and grief abound.

But the parents of those children,
claim our grief and thoughts and tears.
Oh the comfort of reunion,
when eternal light appears.

Author unknown
Supplied by Betty Hueston

Waiting for a Loved One

Anyone who's waiting,
for a loved one to come home.
Will understand just how I felt,
as I paced the floor alone.

The time was long past 3.00 am,
the wind howled at the door.
The rain beat steadily on the panes,
and still I walked the floor.

Our little girl was fast asleep,
tucked in her little bed.
Not old enough to realise,
perhaps her dad was dead.

You see, my man's a policemen,
so he goes out at night.
To do his sworn duty,
to uphold all that's right.

No easy job for any man,
in this awful land of strife.
Just sorrow for his children,
and heartache for his wife.

Not knowing each time he goes out,
if he's ever coming back.
Safely to his family,
or with a bullet in his back.

And this is why I walked the floor,
that awful winter night.
Worried, sad and praying that,
he'd come home all right.

But each time I looked at the clock,
my fears they just increased.
Oh the heartache of a woman,
when her husband's joins the police.

At last relief, I hear the sound,
of car wheels in the drive.
I almost shouted out aloud,
thank God he's home alive.

I ran to meet him at the door,
his face looked very white.
I asked what's wrong and he replied,
my mate's been killed tonight.

I trembled as I listened to,
the words my husband said.
Of how the bullets missed him,
and hit his pal instead.

They'd been on routine patrol,
and everything seemed quiet.
They little knew a gunman,
was hiding in the night.

To do the job his seniors,
had ordered him to do.
To lie in wait and murder,
any policemen in his view.

Then slip away to safety,
when his work was done.
Which makes me stop and wonder,
which of them had won.

The gunman who was safely,
in his hiding place.
Or the young man who had gone,
to be in a better place.

With his precious saviour,
in His loving care.
Where neither bomb nor bullet,
can ever touch him there.

While the man who killed him,
hides in fear and doubt.
Wondering did he hide his tracks,
or will he be found out.

And if by some misfortune,
death should come to him.
What a way to leave this world,
plunged in all that sin.

But if he got the time to ask,
forgiveness for his soul.
And God had kept his name,
written on the roll.

When he'd reach those pearly gates,
and God would say come in.
Would he refuse because he knew,
that policeman was within.

Somehow I don't think so,
'cause Heaven's big enough.
To hold each class and colour,
small and weak and tough.

So when it's possible to be,
with each other there.
Why can't it be the same down here,
and give each man a share.

Of all the little average things,
that makes a normal life.
His work, his home, his parents,
his children and his wife.

Oh please God let this soon be so,
that we can live in peace.
Without this awful nightmare,
'cause a loved one's joined the police.

Author Unknown